CHELSEA AND DERBY CHINA

John Bedford

WALKER AND COMPANY
NEW YORK

Library of Congress Catalog Card Number: LC67–23842

First published in the United States of America in
1967 by Walker and Company, a division of
Publications Development Corporation.

Printed in Hong Kong

Contents

Pair of biscuit figures, a boy and a girl, modelled by George Cocker. c. 1830. 5 in.

Introduction

Whether or not Chelsea was the first English china or porcelain 'manufactory' in date, there can be no doubt as to which was first in quality and widest in range. It was also the only one to earn the approbation of connoisseurs on the Continent—a fact, of course, which leaves amateurs of other English soft-paste factories totally unruffled.

In fact, it did often share the much-loved imperfections of some of these; but I think Chelsea must be accounted unique in the way a group of artists and craftsmen there, some of them foreigners seeking England's traditional asylum, took many of their models from beyond these shores, but expressed them with an English individuality and charm which has not yet faded, and probably never will.

Chelsea handed on its legacy to Derby, and if that factory sometimes faltered in matters of taste, there are ways in which it carried the Chelsea idea to new heights and also made considerable contributions of its own.

In adding this little summary to the Collectors' Pieces series, I have once more to express my appreciation of the work of the specialist students who have preceded me with more complete studies; to thank Mr R. J. Charleston, Keeper of Ceramics at the Victoria and Albert Museum, for permission to take photographs for the colour plates; and to acknowledge very gratefully the sound advice and help given me by Mr John P. Cushion of the same institution.

1. Early Days at Chelsea

If you had lived in London during the eighteenth century and were used to moving around in the world of fashion, you could hardly have escaped falling under the spell of 'the China Ware'. Your hosts would proudly display it in their cabinets, as table services, as containers for sweetmeats and the enticing range of 'desarts' offered you at balls or routs, or—perhaps most splendidly of all—as decorations on the table itself. Here you might see exquisitely modelled figures of shepherds and shepherdesses, beggars, birdsellers and dancers, characters from the stage, gods, goddesses and allegorical figures of all kinds. Once upon a time these had been built up from sugar, dried fruits and paste; but now 'the China Ware' was here, the potter had taken over the confectioners' skill in modelling and colouring.

Continental Europe called these fine wares 'porcelain'. The word came from the Italian *porcellana*, or 'little pig', after a kind of cowrie shell—which the material seemed to resemble in colour and texture. Most of what you saw at that time would have come from the Far East, in the great ships of the East India Companies, but much would have originated in Europe, usually in factories working under the patronage of kings, princes and nobles.

HARD-PASTE PORCELAIN

It would have been of two kinds, quite different in composition and even nature, but each having its own special qualities. The type which came from China and Japan, and also from the German factories, was 'true' porcelain or—to use the term now most widely accepted—'hard-paste'. It had been invented for the first time in China in about the eighth or ninth century AD, and it was made of two forms of felspathic rock—what we now call 'china stone' and 'china clay'.

5

When fired together at an extremely high temperature these two materials fuse and yield a glassy stoneware which rings when struck and is translucent when made thinly. It is a hard, brilliantly white material capable of being thrown on the potter's wheel, cast in moulds, or modelled into the most intricate shapes; and also of being decorated with colours either below a glaze ('underglaze') which is afterwards fired on, or 'enamelled' on the surface of that glaze and fired again to 'fix' these more varied colours.

The secret of this hard-paste porcelain was discovered all over again between the years 1710 to 1715 by a young German alchemist named Johann Friedrich Böttger in collaboration with a German scientist and mathematician, the Ehrenfried Walther von Tschirnhausen, who was economic adviser to Augustus the Strong, Elector of Saxony and King of Poland.

The Saxon monarch not only maintained a vast retinue of mistresses, but had an inordinate passion for Far Eastern porcelain; and Böttger had originally been shut up in a fortress at Meissen, near Dresden, with instructions to solve the alchemical problem and so provide the gold his master so badly needed. But von Tschirnhausen persuaded the Elector to let Böttger try his ingenuity on making porcelain itself: and after some years of experimentation these two eventually worked out a successful formula using local materials.

Thus was born the great porcelain factory of Meissen, which gave a lead to Europe for many years and still exists today. Its products were long known by the name of the Saxon capital itself, but nowadays collectors prefer the term Meissen, to distinguish the wares of the royal factory from those of other establishments which grew up around it.

EUROPEAN SOFT-PASTE

In the meantime potters in France—where there was just as much enthusiasm for the fascinating but fragile wares from the Far East—had come at the problem in quite a different

6

way. Believing that porcelain was some kind of glass, they ground the latter up and mixed it with white clay, lime, soapstone potash, and sometimes bone-ash and other materials.

It was quite a different product from the German and the Chinese. When broken it showed a sugary fracture, instead of the glassy one of the 'true' porcelain, and the glaze was of oxide of lead or tin. The French called it *pâte tendre*—the 'tender paste'—and it was made first at Rouen, about 1673, and in the next century at Chantilly, Saint-Cloud, Mennecy and Vincennes. The last-named factory was subsequently moved to Sèvres where it functioned under the patronage of Madame de Pompadour; and when the secret of hard-paste spread there also in 1768, the 'true' porcelain was made alongside the *pâte tendre*.

Not until somewhere in the early 1740s did an English factory emerge to challenge the porcelain makers of both the East and the Continent. To find it you had to take the road out from Westminster along the King's Private Road to the Royal Hospital, which Charles II had founded to take care of his sick soldiers and sailors. There, among

(Left) *Cream jug in the form of an acanthus leaf. Chelsea, Triangle mark. 5 in.* (Sotheby & Co.) (Centre) *Fluted beaker, decorated with a coloured relief of the flowering tea plant. Chelsea, Triangle period.* $2\frac{7}{8}$ *in.* (Sotheby & Co.) (Right) *Cream jug with relief of coloured floral sprays. Chelsea, Triangle period.* 3·9 *in.* (British Museum.)

market gardens and nurseries, spread along the riverside opposite Battersea, lay the village of Chelsea, famous for its Bun-house, its academies and schools, the wonderful collection of plants and birds in Sir Hans Sloane's Physic Gardens, and as the residence of Swift, Addison and Steele, and a colony of Huguenot craftsmen.

In the year 1742 a chemist named Thomas Briand, who is thought to have been a Frenchman, exhibited before the Royal Society some specimens of what were described in the proceedings as 'a fine white ware made here by himself from native materials of our own country, which appeared to be in all respects as good as any of the finest Porcelane or China Ware'. He claimed that it was 'much preferable too for its fineness to the ware of Dresden, and seemed to answer the character of the true Japan. For when broken it appears like broken sugar, and not like Glass, as the Dresden ware does: and that if it be heated red-hot, and immediately put into cold water, it will not fly or break.' He also attested that 'this ware, before it be glaz'd (a Specimen of which he shew'd) is firm enough to stand the heat of a Glass-house furnace.'

This was undoubtedly a soft-paste of the French type; the problem, still unsolved, is, where Briand made it, and what was his connexion, if any, with the Chelsea factory. It has been guessed that he was a member of the Chelsea Huguenot colony—the Secretary of the Royal Society, who introduced him, lived there—and that perhaps he had been an arcanist, or pottery technician, at some French soft-paste factory such as St Cloud. Some identify him with a Thomas Briand of Derby, who thirty-five years later was modelling porcelain plaques at Bristol.

The next character to appear in the story is a silversmith from Flanders named Nicholas Sprimont. He was born in Liège about the year 1716, and apprenticed there. In 1742, at the age of twenty-six, he entered his name and registered his mark as a silversmith at Goldsmiths' Hall, London, being established in business in Compton Street, Soho.

8

Later that year he was married to a lady named Anne Protin, seemingly a compatriot.

Sprimont was an artist as well as a craftsman, as was shown not very long ago by Mrs Arundel Esdaile, when she discovered in an old album a watercolour, signed by Sprimont, showing a design for a silver dish with two glasses, of which there is a counterpart in porcelain. He occupied the premises in Compton Street, enlarging them from time to time, until 1748; but in the previous year we find him also occupying premises in Chelsea, at the northern end of Laurence Street, his next-door neighbour being Tobias Smollett, the creator of *Roderick Random*.

We do not know who occupied these premises at the time that Briand was making, or having made for him, the 'fine white ware' he showed to the Royal Society, that is to say in the year or two before 1743; for unfortunately the Chelsea rate books for the seven previous years are missing—it is believed that they were taken by some historian who forgot to return them.

There may be a link between him and Sprimont, however, in a document, apparently written by the latter— it is in the Lansdowne MSS at the British Museum—which petitioned the authorities to put a stop to private importations of porcelain from Dresden which were escaping Customs duty. It seems that some highly distinguished persons had been taking advantage of their privileged position to make a profitable racket out of bringing porcelain in their luggage when returning from official or private visits to the Saxon capital. Sprimont claimed that as the Saxon factory was subsidized by royalty, this represented unfair competition for a private venture such as his own—although there is actually some reason for thinking that he enjoyed the patronage, if not of the Duke of Cumberland, at least of that royal prince's secretary, Sir Everard Fawkener.

Sprimont must have been in a fair way of business at the time the petition was written—from internal evidence this must have been between 1745 and 1749—for in spite of difficulties, not only with foreign competition, but also in manufacturing, he said that during the previous winter he had sold china to the value of £3,500 and was at that time employing more than 100 hands, with a nursery of 'thirty lads taken from the parishes and schools and bred to designing and painting'.

The most interesting remark in the petition, however, is where he describes how he came to start up his enterprise. He said that 'from a casual acquaintance with a chymist who had some knowledge this way [he] was tempted to make a trial which, upon the progress he made, he was encouraged to persue with great labour and expense'. Was the 'chymist' Briand: and did he and Sprimont make the 'fine white wares' together?

There is a third character in the story who had definite connexions with Sprimont, and like him was a Huguenot. This was a certain Charles Gouyn, a jeweller, in the parish of St George's, Hanover Square. In 1750 Sprimont mentioned in one of his own sales advertisements that he had no sort of connexion with 'nor for a considerable time has he put any of his ware into that shop in St James' Street which was the Chelsea China Warehouse'. The owner of this retail establishment, a Mr S. Stables, retorted by advertising that 'my China Warehouse is not supply'd by any other person than Mr Charles Gouyn, late Proprietor and Chief Manager of the Chelsea-house, who continues to supply me with the most curious goods of that manufacture, as well as ornamental, and which I dispose of at very reasonable rates'.

Can it be assumed that when Sprimont started to make porcelain at Chelsea, with or without the collaboration of Briand, he was in some kind of partnership with Gouyn? It seems reasonable to suppose that the young silversmith, not long established in his own business, and also recently married, might have found it advantageous, even essential, to team up with a successful trader like Gouyn; but that by about 1748 or 1749 he had become sufficiently well-established to buy out his partner, who perhaps took a good lot of the stock with him to sell to retailers like 'S. Stables'.

But where, one may ask, did Sprimont, a silversmith, get his labourers? Painters he could train, no doubt, but what of the men skilled in throwing at the wheel, in managing the furnaces, in mixing the paste, in making the saggars in which to fire the pieces? Did he take them from the delft-ware makers of Lambeth and elsewhere or the stoneware people out at Fulham, heirs of Dwight?

Or is there truth in a claim by Simeon Shaw, historian of the Staffordshire potteries, to the effect that in about the year 1747 there arrived in Chelsea a team of seven or more Staffordshire men, each trained in his own branch of the potter's craft, who 'started to work at the Chelsea China Manufactory' but, finding that it 'was upon their exertions that all the excellence of the porcelain must depend', they left and commenced business on their own account. If they did work for Sprimont and then leave where did they go: was it to the second china manufactory 'at an old mansion by the riverside' reported by Llewellyn Jewett, a later historian: if so, where are the wares they made? Were they the famous and mysterious 'Girl-in-a-Swing' figures which we shall be looking at shortly?

The person who made off with those rate books has a great deal to answer for.

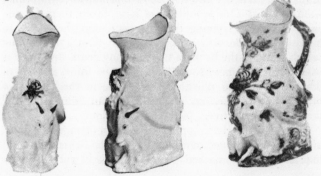

Three Chelsea 'Goat and Bee' jugs, all with incised Chelsea Triangle mark.
(Left) In the British Museum (3·9 in.); (Centre) in the Museum of Art,
Rhode Island School of Design, Providence, R.I. (4$\frac{7}{16}$ in.); (Right)
courtesy of Sotheby & Co. (4$\frac{1}{4}$ in.)

2. The Triangle Wares

The early porcelain makers, as we have seen, thought they were looking for a kind of glass. The milky, highly translucent material of the first of the identifiable Chelsea wares could very easily be mistaken for opaque-white glass of the kind made at Bristol, South Staffordshire and other centres: chemically the two materials are very close to each other. By transmitted light, the body paste shows small flecks or 'pinholes' of greater translucency. The glaze is soft, and almost buttery to the touch.

When a mark was used on these early wares it was usually a triangle—incidentally, the alchemical symbol for fire—and this gives a name to pieces made in this body down to about 1749–50. It is usually incised into the paste, and when there is an accumulation of glaze it can sometimes be difficult to find. Very rarely a piece will bear a crown and trident in the same colour.

GOAT AND BEE JUGS

Quite the most attractive of all the 'triangle' wares, and also the most significant of them for dating, are the famous 'goat and bee' jugs, taken from the silver models of which mention has already been made. There are a surprising number of them in existence and they show unusually accomplished workmanship. One would never have taken them for the early efforts of a young establishment, and they seem to have been made over a longer period than 1745–9. The vessels sit upon the backs of two reclining goats, and there is usually, though not always, a bee on the front, a spray of flowers in applied relief, and a handle in the form of a branch. They may be plain white, but sometimes the flowers are attractively picked out in colour.

The name 'Chelsea' appears on some of them, also a date: and here we have yet another mystery. The British Museum has an example marked with the triangle and the year

(Above) *Chelsea figure of Pu T'ai, the 'Corpulent Monk'. Triangle period. 3⅜ in.* (Sotheby & Co.)
(Right) *Teapot in the form of the 'Fat Chinaman' riding on a parrot. Chelsea, Triangle mark. 7½ in. high.* (Victoria & Albert Museum.)

1745—which seems reasonable enough in view of what we already know. But one specimen, now in the Lucille Pillow Collection at Fredericton, New Brunswick, Canada, bears the triangle, the word 'Chelsea' and apparently the date 1743.

If the date is genuine, the jug is a 'documentary' piece of the first importance. It could be one of the pieces shown by Briand to the Royal Society in that same year as having been 'made here by himself'; or the work of someone who was making soft-paste porcelain at a much earlier date than we usually suppose Sprimont to have been in action. It is possible that Briand, or somebody working to his instructions, may have made these jugs at one of the other factories which are recorded as having been in operation around London at this time, and whose wares have not yet been identified—for example Greenwich or Limehouse. The '3' in the date may be a carelessly made '5'. Alternatively the date may not refer to the year of manufacture of the jug itself but to that on one of the silver originals.

Not surprisingly, in view of their high interest for collectors, the 'goat and bee' jugs have been forged. The late Wallace Elliot, in examining a number of specimens, put them into three groups, one of which he declared 'spurious', believing them to have been made at Coalport. The other two groups, although satisfying the usual requirements as to paste, glaze, etc., showed marked differences in modelling. Lord Fisher suggested that this may well mark two phases in the 'goat and bee' history, one a pre-Sprimont era, the other his partnership with Gouyn, using new models.

DELICATE MODELLING

Some of the other 'triangle' wares also show a complexity and delicacy which one would hardly expect of a beginner in porcelain making. These include the well-known 'crayfish' salts—also having origins in silver—where finely modelled marine creatures and rocks are used as bases. There are also teapots, cups and saucers moulded with overlapping acanthus or strawberry leaves.

Another most attractive family have the delicate applied reliefs called 'raised flowers'—usually a prunus blossom or tea-plant pattern taken from the Chinese—reminiscent of the decoration on the red stonewares made by the Dutch Elers brothers and their Staffordshire potters in the late seventeenth century. Much of this ware has its inspiration in the lovely white porcelain of Te Hua known as *blanc-de-Chine;* but sometimes it has paintings of flower sprays or insects, added in such a way as to conceal flaws in the body.

Similar painting occurs on other shell forms, which may be mounted on a stand of coral with applied shells; there are also versions on a simple fluted foot. The blue triangle appears on some very fine sauce-boats from this period, while some moulded cream jugs and other wares along with the incised triangle bear the as yet unexplained blue crown and trident.

A few very accomplished figures can also be traced to this period. There are the grotesque teapots, showing a fat 'Chinaman' mounted on a snake or a parrot; and at the other end of the aesthetic scale is the very fine 'Rustic Lovers' group, of which there are versions which vary with the degree of boldness shown by the rustic young man.

3. Raised Anchor and Red Anchor

On the evidence of the advertisement already quoted it is usually assumed that Charles Gouyn severed his connexion with the business about the year 1750, leaving Sprimont as proprietor and manager.

By this time the Flemish silversmith, still only in his thirty-fifth year, was evidently well established as a porcelain maker, even having royal patronage. This is suggested by a letter of June, 1751, from Sir Charles Hanbury Williams, British plenipotentiary at the Court of Dresden, to Henry Fox, who was storing his friend's collection of porcelain at Holland House during his service abroad. Sir Charles had been asked by Sir Everard Fawkener, 'who is I believe concerned in the manufacture of China at Chelsea . . . to send over models for different pieces from hence in order to furnish the undertakers with good designs'; but he 'thought it better and cheaper for the manufacturers to give them leave to take any of my China from Holland House and to copy what they like'.

Sir Charles's collection seems to have been a considerable one, and it gave the Chelsea potters plenty of scope for copying. Later, in 1758, Augustus III of Saxony, son of Augustus the Strong, who continued the royal factory, contributed to the collection 'a set of China for a table of thirty covers' which included tea and coffee sets and sweetmeats in the form of artichokes, laurel leaves, sunflowers, etc.

CHELSEA 'MOONS'
About this time there begin to be changes in the composition of the body. It becomes less glassy, stronger, richer in texture. It contains considerably more alumina than the Triangle body, with no lead oxide at all. It has a greenish translucency, showing lighter 'moons' instead of the earlier 'pinpoints'. The next major change occurs when bone-ash,

as used at Bow, was brought into the 'mix' in considerable quantities—as much as forty per cent.

Either to mark the evolution of these improved bodies, or to celebrate his becoming sole proprietor of the factory, Sprimont now adopted a new mark. It was an anchor—nobody knows quite why this particular symbol was chosen—at first in relief on an applied oval medallion (the so-called Raised Anchor) and later painted in red. Very rarely, and usually only on pieces where underglaze blue is used, it appears in blue.

There was considerable overlap in time in the use of these marks—sometimes the Raised Anchor has an outline in red—so that it has become customary to treat them as belonging to the same period. It has been cogently suggested by Mr George Savage that the change from Raised to Red arises from the fact that Sprimont used the Raised Anchor—which could not be tampered with by an outside decorator like Duesbury—to prevent his goods being passed off as the work of others; but that after Duesbury gave up his London decorating shops to go to Derby—which occurred in 1754—it was safe and obviously more convenient to paint the anchor in red.

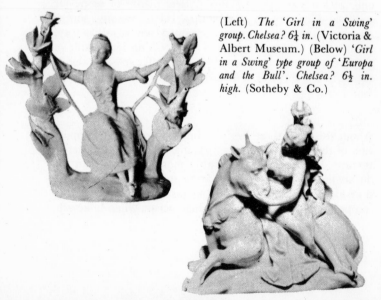

(Left) *The 'Girl in a Swing' group. Chelsea?* $6\frac{1}{4}$ *in.* (Victoria & Albert Museum.) (Below) *'Girl in a Swing' type group of 'Europa and the Bull'. Chelsea?* $6\frac{1}{2}$ *in. high.* (Sotheby & Co.)

Somewhere at the beginning of this period, however, there appears a class of wares whose origin has long puzzled collectors. They are markedly different in many ways from other wares produced at Chelsea, yet they seem to share affinities.

They are named—after one of the most famous and charming of them—the 'Girl in a Swing' class. The body, though similar to that used at Chelsea during the Triangle period, has a much greater content of lead oxide; one of the 'Hurdy Gurdy Boys' shows 17.73 per cent, against 7.5 per cent, not counting the lead in the glaze: this is higher than in any other English soft-paste body except for Longton Hall. According to Mr Savage, who has made the latest count, twenty-four models are known. Some have the raised anchor mark, like the beautiful 'Europa and the Bull' shown here; while one—'Britannia Mourning for the Death of Frederick, Prince of Wales'—gives us a possible clue to the date. 'Poor Fred' died in 1751, and the piece would have been made shortly after this time, in commemoration of his passing without succeeding to his father's throne.

These attractive pieces also have links with one class of the well-known Chelsea 'toys' (see page 36): and it has been proposed that they were the work of another factory altogether, either at Chelsea, or the shadowy establishments at Limehouse and Greenwich. Mr Arthur Lane, in his *English Porcelain Figures of the Eighteenth Century*, after reviewing all the evidence, has suggested that they may be the work of a second Chelsea factory, manned by the seceding Staffordshire workmen already mentioned, and financed by Charles Gouyn. It may have started about the year 1749 and closed in 1754, when its stock could have been taken over by the original factory and offered to the public in the sale of 1754. If this is true, Gouyn must have found—among the Staffordshire hands or elsewhere—a modeller with metropolitan taste and skill and also possessed, as Mr Lane has pointed out, of a rare porcelain sense.

The 'Rustic Lovers' group was made as a member of the 'Girl in a Swing' family as well as in the normal Chelsea style. Such duplication has led to the suggestion that this interesting family represents experimental pieces made at Chelsea—some of them have imperfections acquired during firing in the kiln of the kind which could have occurred in attempts to find a more stable paste. A hidden document or a newly exposed fragment from a waste tip may one day shed light in this dark corner.

EARLY CATALOGUES

Catalogues issued by Sprimont in the years 1755 and 1756 are of great help in studying the wares made down to this date—the 'middle' period of Chelsea production, and for many people its best.

At that date it was customary for manufacturers of luxury articles to build up alongside their 'custom-made' wares large stocks which would on a given date be offered for sale at public auction. Copies of the catalogues of 1755 and 1756 have been preserved, and were reprinted in full respectively in Mr William King's *Chelsea Porcelain* and Mr George Savage's *Eighteenth Century English Porcelain*. Each sale lasted for sixteen days, and the catalogues have been analysed carefully by Mr F. Severne Mackenna in the Red Anchor volume of his trilogy on *Chelsea Porcelain*. His work in aligning the various items with the illustrations of surviving pieces in his own and other books provides fascinating material for the student-collector.

During the first year or two of this era the factory continued to make white wares in imitation of *blanc-de-Chine*, although examples are now very rare. Another outstanding influence at this time—probably derived at second hand through Meissen—was the famous Japanese porcelain from Arita, the Kakiemon wares, named after the family of potters who first established themselves in that district in the seventeenth century.

The Kakiemon wares have characteristic shapes—octagonal, hexagonal or fluted sides are common, and there are bowls with out-turned rims—but their outstanding feature is the painting, both as to style and colour. A very soft and attractive palette is used with a predominating brick red, accompanied by green, blue, turquoise and yellow. Chantilly fell under the spell of this style, and copied specimens for the collection of the Prince de Condé; it was also taken up at Meissen, St Cloud and elsewhere.

KAKIEMON PATTERNS

At Chelsea the designs were copied rather freely; and the artists were perhaps not so daring in their handling of typically Japanese asymmetrical designs. But their work is of great charm, and spectacular use is made of the beautiful white surface of the porcelain—never more attractive at Chelsea than at this time. A number of the patterns listed in the 1755 catalogue may be recognized today; they include the 'tyger and rock', the 'tyger and wheatsheaf', the 'wheatsheaf and pheasant', the 'gnurl'd partridge pattern' and others. The fact that the 'pheasants' were really quails and the 'wheatsheafs' banded hedges need not spoil our enjoyment of these attractive expressions of *Japonaiserie*.

The flood of blue and white porcelain from the Far East which was so freely copied elsewhere in Europe does not seem to have excited Chelsea. On the exceedingly rare specimens known, the anchor mark is also sometimes in blue as already noted. There is one well-known pattern of birds and plants in the Chinese style which is still being sold in modern earthenware; the rare originals are attractively restrained.

Other oriental themes are indicated by the 'India plants' of the catalogues. These could be our old friends the *indianische Blumen* of Meissen—formalized flowers taken from Chinese models. In an age when Chinese and Japanese porcelain came to Europe in the ships of the East India companies, picking up precious commodities from other Asiatic countries on the way, 'Indian flowers' was as near as

(Left) *Plate with cinquefoil rim, painted in underglaze blue in Chinese style with birds, rocks, bamboos, and a trellis diaper border. Diameter 9 in. Chelsea, Blue Anchor mark.* (British Museum.) (Right) *Chelsea botanical plate, painted with* Acacia Americana, *a butterfly and a caterpillar. Red Anchor mark. 8¾ in. diameter* (Sotheby & Co.)

anyone troubled to identify their origin.

The style was strongly developed by Höroldt at Meissen in the generation before Chelsea came into operation, and when, a few years later, this brilliant artistic director of the Saxon factory developed the famous *deutsche Blumen*, or 'German flowers', whereby native plants were given with naturalistic but yet pleasingly stylized faithfulness, Chelsea followed, adding, of course, its characteristic touch.

BOTANICAL PAINTING

The so-called 'Sir Hans Sloane's plants' are in the greatest possible contrast to the spirit of faery which pervaded the *chinoiserie* and rococo themes. Here was an expression of the scientific aspirations of the age. Sir Hans Sloane, a physician from Ulster who had attended Queen Anne, and whose collection became the basis of that of the British Museum, was President of the Royal Society for many years and founded at Chelsea the celebrated Botanical Gardens, based on the original Physic Garden of the Apothecaries' Society. The paintings in Chelsea porcelain are very fine and bold productions in a genre which was continued, rather mechanically and perfunctorily, at Derby and Swansea later on. Many of the subjects appear to be taken from drawings of Philip Miller, the Apothecaries' chief gardener; but others are known to have derived from the engravings of G. D. Ehret.

Designs originating at Meissen—as distinct from those developed there from oriental themes—were given a great deal of attention at Chelsea during this middle period. It has already been stated that Sprimont was helped by Sir Everard Fawkener in obtaining pieces for copying. From this source, presumably, come the charming landscapes and river scenes which are to be found on wares of all kinds, but especially plates and dishes with moulded relief patterns. These were no doubt suggested by the famous harbour scenes—they appear in colour, but also in the crimson monochrome which seemingly is what the catalogues refer to as 'purple landskips'.

'FABLE' PAINTING

This brings us to another of the many puzzles with which collectors beguile themselves—the identity of the painter of the rare and much desired 'Fable' paintings. They occur not only in the Raised and Red Anchor period but also spill over into that of the Gold Anchor. Their subject matter is for the most part taken from one or other of the fabulists whose work was published during the preceding century or so, particularly the *Aesop's Fables* illustrated by Francis Barlow, which came out in various editions from 1687 onwards.

'Fable' teapot, painted in colours by Jeffrey Hamet O'Neale. Chelsea. (City Museum, Stoke-on-Trent.)

Chelsea basket-moulded dish, finely painted with a landscape in the Vincennes style. Raised Anchor period. $10\frac{1}{4}$ in. long. (Sotheby & Co.)

Stylistically there appear to have been at least two 'Fable' painters. The chief one proposed is the Jeffrey Hamet O'Neale about whom almost as many controversial things have been written as there are ways of spelling his Christian names. The facts we know about this almost legendary character are few. He was an outside decorator—the English equivalent of the Continental *Hausmaler*—who exhibited miniatures, and around 1765 was working in a studio in London. Around the years 1768–70 he was living in Worcester, decorating and signing work for the factory there. This work is much heavier-handed than that of the 'Fable' painting, and if it is the work of the same man there must have been a steep deterioration in his standards. But it seems now to be generally accepted that at least some of the 'Fable' painting is his.

The name of William Duvivier has been proposed for the earlier work. Like Sprimont himself, Duvivier was a native of Liège; he worked at Tournai and came to England about 1743, dying there in 1755. It is thought by Mr Savage that he may have worked under and been instructed by O'Neale. A third candidate for the 'Fable' painter is Jean Lefebre, later also associated with Tournai, who had a child

22

born in Chelsea in 1761, but is supposed to have lived there much earlier.

Whoever painted the earlier 'Fables' had a delightful touch which is also to be seen in some of the landscapes and animal subjects. As to their placing, they are perhaps most happily used when they appear in the panels of the moulded wares already mentioned. One excellent example is the pattern known as the Warren Hastings service, after a set once owned by that statesman.

SILVER-STYLE MOULDINGS

Most of these mouldings are, of course, taken from silver originals, and in fact are often referred to in the catalogues as 'chased'—an example of silversmiths' terms creeping, not inappropriately, into porcelain. This one probably refers to those extremely rococo plates where the high relief mouldings break out into a riot of scrolls and asymmetrical curves. The expression 'damask'd' or 'damask work'd' also occurs in the catalogues, and this perhaps describes (again quite appropriately) the type of moulding which has delicate flower mouldings around the rims—but which the painter sometimes ignores in the placing of his flowers and insects. The 'Warren Hastings' is perhaps the so-called 'moulded' pattern but it is not very clear what is meant by either 'mosaic' or 'gnurl'd'. There is also basket moulding,

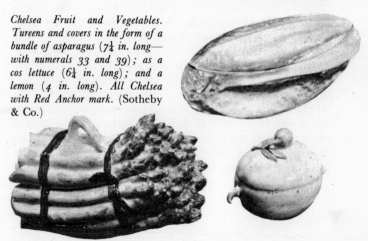

Chelsea Fruit and Vegetables. Tureens and covers in the form of a bundle of asparagus (7¼ in. long— with numerals 33 and 39); as a cos lettuce (6¼ in. long); and a lemon (4 in. long). All Chelsea with Red Anchor mark. (Sotheby & Co.)

Chelsea Birds. A pair of Flycatchers painted in colours (4 in. high; Raised Anchor marks); and a 'Girl in a Swing' type canary, painted in colours. 2½ in. (Sotheby & Co.)

sometimes with vine leaves superimposed, or the feather scroll edging which one encounters more often in the later periods.

Painting and modelling are seen together on a class of wares decorated with what are called 'applied flowers'. They include cups, tureens and sauce-boats with flowers and leaves in relief around their forms, and having twig handles. Their colours are pleasing, and although deriving from Meissen, they are often more beautiful than the originals. A relief decoration of scolopendrium leaves, though not always successful, seems to come off very well on a teapot form in the Raised Anchor period.

ANIMAL AND VEGETABLE
Modelling 'in the round', also accompanied by fine painting, is seen in a family of tureens, boxes and other 'useful' wares made in the forms of fruit, vegetables, animals and birds; they have been very grandly described as the 'phytomorphic' and the 'zoomorphic' wares. There are

24

cauliflowers which take apart—and (like those in our gardens) have butterflies perched upon them: there are bundles of asparagus, lettuces, artichokes, melons, lemons, apples, red and white cabbages, figs, grapes, pears, pomegranates, pineapples, roses, and sunflowers. The livestock department includes boar's heads, drakes and ducks of various breeds, gamecocks, hens and chickens, partridges, pigeons (sometimes doubled), rabbits, and extremely beautiful swans. Fish include carp, eels, plaice: the turtle is also seen in the land.

To judge by the prominence these items are given in the catalogues, and the glowing terms in which they are described, they must have been tremendously popular, and

Chelsea Bird Tureens. (Left) *Partridge ($5\frac{1}{2}$ in.; Red Anchor mark and numeral 50 on both cover and base—a rare event).* (Sotheby & Co.) (Right) *Hen and Chickens on a stand decorated with sunflowers, as described in the catalogue. $9\frac{7}{8}$ in. high.* (Victoria & Albert Museum.)

Chelsea figure of a beggar, attributed to Joseph Willems. Red Anchor period. 7⅜ in. (Sotheby & Co.)

indeed a great many have survived—which perhaps also suggests that they were not always regarded as 'useful' wares. The modelling is extremely good, often, where there is one, surpassing the Meissen original; and much ingenuity is shown in the selection of features for a handle or the division of vessel and lid. The colouring is often superb.

Many of them, however, have lost their stands, which were often as ingenious as the rest. The hen with her chicks, for example, originally fluffed herself out upon a platform of sunflower leaves and blossoms. This is revealed by the catalogue of 1755 which refers to 'A most beautiful tureen in the shape of a "hen and chickens", big as the life, in a curious dish adorn'd with sunflowers'. The carp rests upon a basket-moulded stand with water plant leaves; the partridge has a nest with wheat-ears. There seem to be no clues to the modeller or modellers responsible for these engaging things.

CHELSEA FIGURES

Modelling and painting at Chelsea reaches its apogee with the wonderful range of ornamental figures. They are among the very finest productions of the kind ever made in England, and, like the 'toys' shortly to be discussed, are among the few English porcelain wares to have earned Continental approbation. As has been conceded by Dr Robert Schmidt, Director of the Schlossmuseum, Berlin, the models, though not necessarily original, are sometimes better *modelled* than

26

the originals. Their material, too, has a quality which was never surpassed anywhere in soft-paste—and to many tastes is to be preferred even to the hard-paste of Europe.

In the Raised Anchor wares, figures made after the *blanc-de-Chine* of Te Hua continued in production alongside the 'useful' wares of this type. Sometimes they are literal copies, like the figures of the goddess Kuan Yin, that very pleasant character who would even pause on her way into Heaven to rescue some unfortunate person.

There are also enchanting adaptations in the mood of *chinoiserie*. This fantastical and playful view of life in a faraway land of romance and faery had little to do with the actual art or life of the Far East. Most of the ideas were derived from European artists like Jean Pillemont and they were taken up strongly at Meissen. Chelsea, however, seems often to have preferred to go to the original engravings rather than the Meissen derivations. There are also subjects from Boucher, such as *Les Delices de l'Enfance*, a group in two parts, where a separate little Chinese boy has to be placed alongside his mother and brother.

In the white also are some busts of royal or otherwise famous persons: Peg Woffington, the famous actress, appears as the head of a sphinx, while the Duke of Cumberland, Sprimont's royal patron—if that is what he was—is also given a bust. There are heads of children, one of which

'Leda and the Swan.' Red Anchor mark. Chelsea. c. 1755. The subject is adapted from a painting by François Boucher, first exhibited in 1742 and now in the National Museum, Stockholm. (Victoria & Albert Museum.)

was once thought to be Sophie Roubiliac, daughter of the famous sculptor (also a god-daughter of Sprimont's) but is now believed to have been modelled after Fiammingo—and some of the other busts have been traditionally attributed to him. The idea that certain later pieces marked with an 'R' are his, is, however, no longer generally accepted; they are probably from Bow.

Most charming of all these white figures, perhaps—though also to be found in colours—is the 'Chellsea Nurse', the delightful nurse and child originally modelled by Barthelmy de Blénod and made at the Avon Pottery, near Fontainebleau, in the seventeenth century. In contrast with this are the much less lovely court dwarfs, after engravings by Jacques Callot; and in the same way the hideous *Affenkapelle*, or Monkey Band, supposed to be a satire on the Dresden Court Orchestra, is surely as out of place in Chelsea porcelain as it was in that of Meissen: the grotesque seems to be more at home in stoneware.

Among the coloured figures, perhaps the most outstandingly skilled are those from the Italian Comedy. Beautifully modelled, and with the most sparing use of flat washes of colour, these figures also are sometimes more appealing aesthetically than the Meissen or other models from which they are taken. Based on the characters of the *Commedia dell'Arte*, they represent the mockery, irony, charm and sentimentality of the popular Renaissance stage. The entertainment was of great antiquity, and survives even today in the work of the Piccola Scala Company in Milan.

As might be expected in the eighteenth century, Chelsea was required to produce its quota of classical and allegorical figures. Gods and goddesses like Mars and Venus, Diana and Ceres, Mercury, Jupiter, Juno and others appear, usually on rather larger models (say ten to fourteen inches high) than is perhaps appropriate to porcelain. This also applies to some models of the Senses (Sight, Smell, Touch, etc.) which again are thought to have possibly been the work of a sculptor rather than of a porcelain modeller. With the 'Leda and the Swan' shown here, however, one returns to proper ceramic proportions, and the effect is excellent. So is it, too, with the smaller versions of the Seasons.

Mr Lane attributes a great many of the Chelsea figures of this time to Joseph Willems, a modeller from Brussels who worked at Chelsea from about 1749 to 1766.

There are not a great many religious figures, as one might expect of an English factory, though among them is a charming Madonna and Child, some monks and nuns, also an ambitious *Pieta*. Children often appear embodying allegorical ideas, such as the Arts and Sciences, the Continents, and also the 'Cupids in Disguise', used in services.

Much of the most attractive modelling was done as decoration for candlesticks, flower-holders and the like, or to contain 'desarts' or sweetmeats. There are Turkish figures holding shells, and the really splendid pair of the 'Man and Woman seated beside Baskets' which was illustrated in colour by Mr King.

Red Anchor charm and skill, and an interesting commentary on eighteenth-century attitudes, are also shown in the ordinary people featured in the models. There are peasants—often performing country dances—carpenters, pedlars, map-sellers, fishermen, cooks, gardeners and ratcatchers. Hurdy-gurdy players appear, as well as ballad singers and performers on that extraordinary instrument the salt-box, of which no less a person than Dr Johnson was an admirer.

CHELSEA BIRDS

Birds were produced in great quantities during the Raised Anchor period but few are mentioned in the 1755 catalogue. Once again the idea—or rather the fashion—came from Meissen: that factory itself had been strongly influenced by Chinese originals dating from the reign of K'ang Hsi.

But many of the Chelsea models seem to have been taken direct from plates in George Edwards's *Natural History of British Birds*, first published in 1743. This artist is quoted on one occasion as having complained that the porcelain makers were filling the shops with birds 'after the figures in my History of Birds which are sadly misrepresented as to shape and colouring'. Certainly the painting is not always naturalistic; and in fact some of these birds seem, in one commentator's phrase, to have put themselves into fancy dress. Nevertheless the members of the Chelsea aviary at this time are extremely engaging, and collectors eagerly search for the blue-tits, whip-poor-wills, barn owls, ptarmigans, ducks, finches, geese, hens, harriers, parrots, doves, woodpeckers, canaries and the rest. Many of them were probably painted by the 'outside enameller' William Duesbury, of whom a great deal more will be heard later.

Many more Raised and Red Anchor figures are to be found than can be described in this little book. They represent a very notable contribution to English ceramics and in their own line they have never quite been surpassed.

Architectural watch stand representing 'The Dawn of Day', the watch with movement by Edward Webb. 10½ in. high. Chelsea, Red Anchor mark. (Sotheby & Co.)

4. Gold Anchor

At some time towards the end of 1756 Sprimont seems to have run into the first of his bouts of severe illness. The *Public Advertiser* for 15 February 1756–7 carried the following announcement: 'The Public is hereby acquainted that the Chelsea Porcelain Factory has been very much retarded by the Sickness of Mr Sprimont; Nevertheless, several curious Things have been finished, which will be exposed to Sale at the Warehouse in Piccadilly, some time the Beginning of March, of which more particular Notice will be given.'

A fourteen-day sale was held in Dublin in the spring of 1758, while in 1759, the *Public Advertiser* carried a notice to the effect that a Mr Burnsall would offer for sale at his Great Auction Room in Charles Street, Berkeley Square, by order of Mr Sprimont, the Proprietor of the Chelsea Manufactory 'all the valuable and very Curious last new Production of his very beautiful Chelsea Porcelain; consisting of some matchless blue and gold Vauses, Perfume-Pots, large Cabinet two-handled Cups and Covers, some Pot-Pourri and other Pieces of the Pea Green and Gold, never before exhibited; some beautiful large groups, and single Figures for Brackets with many other Articles for Table, Tea and Coffee services: the Whole most delicately enamel'd in Figures, Birds, Flowers, etc.'

There is more than a hint here of a considerable change in the style of the wares being produced, especially in such terms as 'Pieces of the Pea Green and Gold never before exhibited'. This is confirmed in the catalogue of another sale in the following year, when, after describing the several kind of wares being offered, there were also '. . . for the Approbation of the Connoisseur, a few Pieces of some new Colours, which have been found this year by Mr Sprimont, the Proprietor, at a very large Expense, incredible Labour, and close finished and heightened with the Gold peculiar to that fine and distinguish'd Manufactory, which makes this

Porcelain the most Beautiful and magnificent ever seen, and cannot be made at any Foreign Manufactory.'

These were bold claims, but there does from now on appear a new magnificence in the styles and decoration. The body is fully bone-ash in type, and the restrained work of the Raised and Red Anchor period has given place to new exotic ground colours and lavish gilding, to grandly conceived forms and much elaborate applied work.

SEVRES INFLUENCE

It has been suggested that during his temporary retirement Sprimont may have taken a 'cure' somewhere on the Continent, perhaps at one of the French spas, for from now on we find the influence of Sèvres gradually displacing that of Meissen. That factory, so long the main source of inspiration for all the other European factories, had run into trouble of its own, having fallen into the hands of the Prussians at the outbreak of the Seven Years War and been leased by Frederick the Great to his army-contractor. From this date on it worked under great difficulties, and slowly lost the lead in porcelain-making to its French rival at Sèvres, which was now enjoying royal favour.

NEW COLOURS

The new Chelsea colours announced in 1760 seem to have been the turquoise (the *bleu celeste* of Sèvres) and the 'crimson' of the catalogue. This was presumably what we know as claret, uniquely Chelsea's though based on the famous Sèvres *rose Pompadour*—not *rose du Barry* as it is often called in England: that lady did not appear at Court until 1769. These were notable additions to the early yellow ground, the pea-green of the previous year, and the rich, vibrant 'mazarine blue' already in use. There seems nothing to associate the name of this colour with Cardinal Mazarin: one wonders if it had to do with the Countess Mazarine who appears to have been living in Chelsea at the time. These colours were also seen in reticulated or scale versions.

32

Gilding now appears everywhere, for we are in the era of the Gold Anchor, which starts to be used about the year 1758, although occasionally it appears in red (in a 'pointed' version) and also in brown.

The gilding is now carried out by a new procedure: no longer is leaf gold ground up with honey: a richer effect is given by making an amalgam of gold and mercury, then grinding this into a fusible glaze so that it can be fired on to the ware more thickly, then burnished and chased into a brilliance impossible with the older method. In one very striking class of so-called 'gold ground' wares there are Meissen-style figures, flowers and exotic birds, also painting in brilliant colours against a gold field, rather as in some kinds of lustre ware.

Elaborate painting, too, is the order of the day. Magnificent work was done even on tea and table wares—for example the very fine tea service donated to the Victoria and Albert Museum by Mrs Emily R. Thomson, of Dover. It shows figure painting described in the catalogue as being after Watteau (but much more likely to have been based on the *chinoiserie* of Pillement) in reserved panels in a claret ground with the most delicate gilding.

A famous service was made to the order of Queen Charlotte for her brother the Duke of Mecklenburg-Strelitz; reserved panels with flowers are set in a ground of mazarine blue painted with gilt insects. Magnificent as it was—a pair of candelabra from the service is in the Schreiber Collection in the Victoria and Albert Museum—it did not earn the

Pair of 'Fable' candlesticks with bocage. (Left) 'The Cock and Jewel'. (Right) 'The Vain Jackdaw', 10½ in. high. (Centre) Vase moulded in relief and gilt on a dark mazarine blue ground. All Chelsea, Gold Anchor period. 12¼ in. high. (Victoria & Albert Museum.)

approval of Horace Walpole. After mentioning that it cost twelve hundred pounds he wrote of it to a friend: 'I cannot boast of our taste; the forms are neither new, beautiful nor various. Yet Sprimont, the manufacturer, is a Frenchman. It seems their taste will not bear transplanting.' Perhaps he did not realize how necessary it was for Sprimont not to be too adventurous in offering French styles for English consumption.

By way of contrast, the mould of the Mecklenburg-Strelitz service, with a slight difference in the relief panels, is used for fruit painting on a service made for the Duke of Cambridge: a plate from this service is in the Victoria and Albert Museum. Another of the simpler styles of the time shows attractive painting in black with a green wash carried over it; the subjects are sometimes local views, freely taken from engravings. This work is perhaps from the studio of the 'outside decorator' James Giles: there seem to be stylistic links with his 'dishevelled birds' as seen on the porcelain of Bow and Worcester. The black and green painting also appears at those factories.

IMARI PATTERNS

At this time there is also a revival—perhaps in the most acceptable form ever made in England—of the imitations or adaptations of the second sort of wares from Arita, the so-called 'brocaded Imari', echoing designs on the silks and brocades of the Far East. This may perhaps be identified with the 'scollop'd dishes, fine old japan pattern, *blue and gold*' of the 1756 catalogue. Here again, the work at Chelsea was a great improvement on the original, both in design and colour.

Almost too overwhelming in their splendour of potting and decoration are the *garnitures de cheminées* of the period. In these large vases, made in sets like those of China, the rococo is in full flood, with mouldings of loops, scrolls and piercings and with applied flowers of life size. Rich gilding makes the greatest possible use of the coloured grounds, with panels of meticulous painting after Watteau, Pillement, Boucher and other painters of classical and allegorical subjects. On some vases the gilding is almost encrusted on: witness a set of three, one of which is shown on page 33, is moulded with vine leaves, grapes, insects and branches, all heavily gilt on the mazarine blue ground.

GOLD ANCHOR FIGURES
Figures have now moved strongly into the rococo. In such groups as the 'Music Lesson', based on an engraving after Boucher called *L'Agréable Leçon*, the decoration known as *bocage*—meticulously modelled flowers and foliage—surrounds the figures. In this case it is a flowering haw-thorn, and the gilt rococo-scrolled base is decorated with other applied flowers. Our picture shows this group between two others with which it forms a *garniture*: one group represents 'Winter and Spring', the other 'Summer and Autumn'. *Bocage* was also greatly used on items such as candlesticks, like the pair shown on page 33. These groups illustrate two of Aesop's Fables, 'The Cock and the Jewel' and 'The Vain Jackdaw'; and they will perhaps be the 'pair of Fable candlesticks' or 'pair of toilette candlesticks. fable

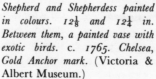
Shepherd and Shepherdess painted in colours. 12⅝ and 12¼ in. Between them, a painted vase with exotic birds. c. 1765. Chelsea, Gold Anchor mark. (Victoria & Albert Museum.)

pattern' of the 1770 catalogue. The flowering hawthorn is used again here, also the rococo base on three feet. There are also some charming small 'family groups'.

The very spirit of the age is seen in the 'shepherd and shepherdess' shown on page 35. Here obviously, with an elegance never known to any real shepherd or shepherdess of sheep, are a disguised lady and gentleman, the one with a rose in her hand and a basket of flowers, displaying her flowered petticoat and red shoes, the man offering flowers with all the exquisite graces required at Vauxhall or Ranelagh. Nothing could better express that desire, so characteristic of the rococo era, to escape from the realities of life into the supposed—or half pretended—simplicities of the bucolic life. A few years later Marie Antoinette was herself to play at milkmaids with her ladies at Malmaison.

Broader effects are aimed at in the large figures such as a set of 'Apollo and the Muses', 'Una and the Lion' and others. Some of these are thought to be the work of Joseph Willems.

Chelsea scent bottle of Italian Comedy inspiration, made in the 'Girl in a Swing' tradition, with Harlequin and Columbine. The base is inscribed 'LE MISTAIRE EST CHARMANS'. 3¾ in. (Sotheby & Co.)

CHELSEA 'TOYS'

As far back as 1754 Sprimont had devoted an entire sale to the small objects which have become known as 'Chelsea Toys', perhaps as the result of his taking over the 'Girl in a Swing' factory. Of all the Chelsea products these pretty trifles have earned the greatest admiration abroad: they even achieved a mention in Beaumarchais' *Marriage of Figaro*, on which Mozart's opera was based. Sometimes they are simply small figures like the 'Cupids Disguis'd', where

(Right) *Chelsea peacock scent bottle, painted in colours and with gold mounts, Red Anchor period.* 3½ in. (Sotheby & Co.) (Below) *Scent bottle modelled as a boy catching birds. Under the base the motto 'JE VIS EN ESPERANCE'. Chelsea.* c. *1765.* (Victoria & Albert Museum.)

these small emblems of love appear in various characters—doctor, soldier, vivandière, nurse, beggar, lawyer, drummer, and the like. They were intended to stand among the 'desart' dishes, and many of them are taken from Meissen originals. Then there are a great many miniature figures of all kinds—sportsmen, gardeners, with wheelbarrows or lawnmowers, gallants and ladies, soldiers. Most of them are no more than 2 to 2½ in. in height.

Alongside these are the pieces which have a function—if the word can be used of such exquisite trifles. They served as thimble cases, seals, bonbonnières, scent bottles, needle-

cases, and the like: seals seem to outnumber all other pieces. Some of these 'toys' bear inscriptions in a quaint anglicized French. A patch-box in the form of a basket of fruit shows a ribbon with the motto L'AMOUR LES A CUEILLI POUR LA PLUS BELLE; a scent-bottle has two flaming hearts outlined in gold and the words: JE TIRE AU COEUR; another, modelled as the pug-dog so popular in that day, has the word AFIDELLE. From the 'weekly bills' kept by Barton it appears that many of them were painted by Boreman and a Willems or 'Williams'—apparently a brother of Willems the modeller although 'Wollams and Co' suggests an 'outside decorating' firm. These toys were exported all over Europe, outselling the native productions, as Lady Charlotte Schreiber found when she travelled around on those china-hunting expeditions of hers which have left us such a priceless legacy in the famous Collection at the Victoria and Albert Museum.

5. Early Derby

Porcelain making began in Derby, it seems, a few years before 1750. This date appears on one of three surviving documentary cream jugs, of indifferent quality, decorated with applied strawberries and leaves. One, in the British Museum, has the initial 'D'; a second, in the Victoria and Albert Museum, shows the inscription 'D.1750'; and the third, in a private collection, has the word 'Derby' incised.

There is a shadowy legend about a foreigner having made small animal figures in a pipe-maker's kiln in Derby as early as 1745. The late Frank Hurlbutt illustrated one of these, and claimed it as the work of one Andrew (or André) Planché; as the result of which considerable speculation has followed without a great deal of new evidence.

Planché, who was born in London in 1728, was said to have learned his trade at Meissen: another version says that his father worked there. He seems to have been living in Derby in 1751, for in that year he had a son baptised in the town. He was presumably still living there in 1756, for in that year two more sons were baptized, one by his wife and the other illegitimate. From this circumstance he has been judged to have led a dissolute life—which seems to be taking things rather for granted.

Planché modelled a series of groups like the 'Boy Milking a Goat', in the Victoria and Albert Museum, and the 'Florentine Boars' and 'Bulls' in the Derby Museum. They are taken from bronze or marble originals in Italy, and in feeling are totally continental—the very last kind of thing one would expect from a small new factory remotely tucked away in the English provinces. Near relatives of these are some *chinoiserie* groups like those seen in R. L. Hobson's catalogue of the British Museum collection. The Schreiber Collection's 'Lady with the Basket' is another of the series which seems to have affinities with other attested Derby pieces.

Pair of boars painted in tones of brown and black. Derby. c. *1753. 6 in. long.* (Sotheby & Co.)

'DRY-EDGE' FIGURES

These figures have become known as the 'dry-edge' class, because the edge of the base is left clear of glaze, as though it were not completely dipped; and in some the vent hole in the base—through which the gases escaped during firing—is screw-shaped.

There is in existence a deed of partnership which, though unsigned, suggests that an enterprise was set afoot about the year 1756 bringing together, in an earthenware pottery at Cockpit Hill, Andrew Planché, described as a 'china maker'; William Duesbury, 'of Longton, in the county of Stafford, enameller' (of whom we have already heard); John Heath, a Derby banker who was at that time a partner with William Butts, a potter; and Thomas Rivett, M.P. for the town. Heath put £1,000 into the venture, and Duesbury raised his share from his father, a currier of Longton, by guaranteeing his parent food and shelter for the rest of his life—a pact he scrupulously observed.

William Duesbury was born in Longton, Staffordshire, about 1725. He opened his china-decorating establishment in London about the year 1751, and as well as doing work for other factories he was, as we have seen, responsible for decorating a good deal of the Chelsea wares made by Sprimont in those years. Mr Savage has cogently suggested that this circumstance may be responsible for the virtual absence of underglaze blue—a factory process—which we have noted at Chelsea: it would have been more convenient for Sprimont, with limited resources in his early years, to rely only on Duesbury's enamelling kilns for decoration of his wares.

DUESBURY AS DECORATOR

Duesbury's *London Account Books*, which were transcribed by Mrs McAlister and published by the English Porcelain Circle, are of great interest to collectors for the clues they give as to his work on the Chelsea wares: they seem to include birds, dogs and other animals, also 'boys with basons'. But the orthography of these books sometimes runs a little wild: a crane is first mistaken for an ostrich and then rendered 'hostorredg', owls are 'houls', women are 'Whiming', and an artichoke is a 'harty choke'. 'Flapwing birds, Chelsey ps'hesons, cocktail birds' might have baffled even Sir Hans Sloane.

Perhaps because of shortage of orders from the potteries—it will be recalled that Sprimont was training his own 'nursery' of boy decorators at this time, and no doubt other factories were following suit—Duesbury in about 1754 went back to Longton, where he seems to have been associated for a time with William Littler at the Longton Hall factory. Littler was the only porcelain maker in Staffordshire at that time and no doubt it was either for him or for one of the salt-glazed stoneware manufacturers that Duesbury had been enamelling the 'Stafartshire' figures mentioned in the *Account Books*.

In these years he was also enamelling 'Derby figars' —apparently the 'dry-edge' pieces made by John Heath and his partners, perhaps modelled by André Planché, at the Cockpit Hill pottery. Some were painted in fired enamels, some in 'cold' oil colours—a practice which may

Chinoiserie group representing 'Feel-ing' from a set of the Senses, Derby 'dry-edge' type. 9½ in. (Sotheby & Co.)

well account for the large number of pieces which appear to have been left in the white, or where only partial colouring survives.

It is generally supposed that such porcelain as was made in Derby before this date would have been fired at Cockpit Hill, but that about the date of the agreement, the enter-prise took new premises in Nottingham Road. Here, per-haps, was made the porcelain which was offered in the same year to the fashionable world in London, according to the following advertisement printed by Edward E. Hyam in *The Early Period of Derby Porcelain:*

RICHMOND WELLS IN SURREY
On Monday next there will be a Ball at the large Assembly-Rooms. It being the full of the Moon, there are expected many Persons of Quality and Distinction: and as it is thought this Assembly will be very numerous and brilliant, the Doors will be open'd at Five O'clock. To be sold by Hand at the said Rooms a large Quantity of China and Japan both useful and ornamental; complete and other sets of fine India dressing-boxes; a large quan-tity of India-Fans, in the newest Taste; the greatest variety of the Derby Porcelain, in Figures, Jars, Candle-sticks; Sauce-Boats, Fruit-Baskets, Lettices, Leaves, Roses, and several curious Pieces for Desserts, finely

41

enamelled in Dresden Flowers, reckoned by Judges who have been Purchasers, to excel in, if not exceed, any Thing of the kind in England.

It will be noted that 'Derby Porcelain' apparently needed no introduction to the world which came to balls at this fashionable watering-place and spa on the edge of London—whither, it is interesting to reflect, Sprimont was to move after his illness in 1762. Later that same year a three-day sale 'by order of the Proprietors of the Derby Porcelain Manufactory' was held in Cavendish Square, London, again offering a variety of pieces 'after the finest Dresden models'.

From this it is evident that the Derby factory at this date was in full production, and also that it was in a position to offer wares in the currently fancied styles of Meissen. One may assume therefore that, whatever his financial interest, Duesbury, with first-hand knowledge of the public's requirements gained from his retail connexions, was now in charge of the factory.

In the year 1757 another sale was held in London, and this time Duesbury was confident enough to refer in his advertisement to 'Derby, or the Second Dresden' and to claim of his figures that 'many good judges could not distinguish them from the real Dresden'.

The earliest of the identifiable groups of figures in this period, perhaps made even before 1756 and up to about 1760, have been called by Mr Honey the 'pale-coloured family', from the hues used and the relative lack of gilding. In subjects and style they fulfil the promise of the 'second Dresden' in the catalogue, and they were apparently intended to compete with Chelsea Red Anchor figures. Once considered to be Bow productions, they are lively, vivacious figures, having something of the charm of miniatures, and perhaps are the most attractive of any from Derby. The Victoria and Albert Museum has several

'Woman Carrying a Hen' and 'Man Carrying a Cock'. Derby 'patch' family; $8\frac{1}{2}$ *and* $8\frac{13}{16}$ *in.* (Museum of Art, Rhode Island School of Design, Providence, R.I.)

examples—a pair of 'Turkish Dancers', a 'Lady Playing a Lute', and a 'Flute Player'. The 'Lovers with a Clown' is after a well-known Meissen original.

THE 'PATCH' FAMILY

Some of these pieces have on their bases three or four dark patches which have been left clear of the glaze and so have become discoloured: they are from the stilts or pads of clay on which the figures stood during their time in the glazing kiln. These marks are sometimes, though very rarely, seen also on the wares of other factories. They are, however, far more commonly seen on a later class known as the 'Patch' family. These were once ascribed to Chelsea or Bow, but in an historic article in the *Burlington Magazine* in 1926 they were shown by Bernard Rackham, Herbert Read and W. B. Honey to have affinities with later marked figures of undoubted Derby origin, and also to differ in phosphatic content from the wares of the London factories.

The subjects are again largely Meissen's but the treatment is highly individual. There is, too, a strong family likeness which suggests the work of a single modeller. They are not in the least like the Chelsea figures of the time—the heads are rounded, the noses sharply pointed, and there is a characteristic bright red spot on the cheeks: the type has an attractive doll-like quality. Examples of them in the

'*Europa and the Bull*'. *Derby* '*patch*' *family.* c. *1765.* (Victoria & Albert Museum.)

Figures of 'The Seasons' modelled after Meissen originals by Eberlein. Derby. 1760–65. 9½ to 10½ in. (Sotheby & Co.)

Schreiber Collection include a pair of 'Minuet Dancers', a 'Youth and Girl with a Performing Dog', a group of 'Hurdy Gurdy Players' after Vanloo. There are exact copies of Meissen figures, like the 'Man carrying a Cock' and the 'Woman carrying a Hen'; there are also English-style figures of Milton, Shakespeare and Britannia. A number of pastoral figures are fitted out as candlesticks, with elaborate *bocage*.

The 'useful wares' of the period are not very plentiful. There are cups and saucers, teapots and punch-pots, sauce-boats on trays. Most attractive of them, I think, are the small salts and sweetmeats baskets, some of which are shown by Mr Gilhespy in his *Derby Porcelain*.

The hands of several painters are apparent. One painted flowers with tendril-like stalks also seen on the 'Diana' at the Victoria and Albert Museum. Another was the 'moth-painter' who gave these and other Meissen insects a fresh treatment and was also responsible for some rather summarily painted birds and landscapes which appear on coffee pots and jugs and pierced vases. The hand of other painters is seen in some cherry subjects and also a combination of a tulip and a rose, as pointed out and illustrated by Mr

Gilhespy. In the Schreiber Collection are some Kakiemon-style flowers and banded hedges in crimson monochrome.

The palette used, as might be expected, has decided similarities with that used for the figures. There is the distinctive turquoise green, which has often become discoloured and dirty, but one also notes delicate tints for the flower patterns on the clothes of the figures. The small sauce-boats have their overlapping leaves edged in green with pink on the handles; there are also brown edges on many of the wares.

In general, however, the 'useful' wares of this era must be regarded as the prelude for the splendid outburst of production in this class which occurred during the later periods.

'Pensent-ils Au Raisin?' after an engraving from a painting by Boucher. Chelsea-Derby. c. 1770? 8¼ in. high. (Victoria & Albert Museum.)

6. Chelsea–Derby

William Duesbury and his banker partner took over the Chelsea factory on 5 February, 1770. For the next fourteen years both establishments were under his control, and although Bow struggled on alone for another five years, Duesbury may be said to have inherited the trade of that factory also. From then onwards the entire artistic policy of both establishments was decided by the ex-decorator's acute business sense—a very different matter from Sprimont's cultivated flair and *esprit*.

Although porcelain was both potted and decorated in either place, it seems likely by the size of the respective factories that most of the potting was done at Derby and most of the decorating at Chelsea. It is, however, extremely difficult—and perhaps not of any great importance—to decide exactly where the work was done. For this reason the wares of the two establishments at this period are usually known as 'Chelsea-Derby'—although stylistically it would perhaps be more appropriate to follow Mr King's example and call them 'Derby-Chelsea'.

'HANTIKE VAUSES'

Duesbury installed as his foreman the modeller Richard Barton, who sent his master at Derby 'weekly bills' of wages and other disbursements. They show that the whole range of porcelain making went on there, from modelling and firing wares in the kiln to 'repairing' (assembling) figures, chasing and polishing (burnishing); even to 'making of TryHangles for the work to be passed on in the Glasd kiln'. Barton seems to have gone to the same school as the man who had kept Duesbury's *London Account Books* of 1751–4, for the items enumerated ranged from '6 Turks a Smoakin' to 'Hantike Vauses, with 3 figures each'.

The team at Chelsea included three labourers named Inglefield, Piggot, and Roberts, who cut up cordwood for the kilns, made saggars or clay boxes in which the wares were fired, ground up, trod and 'bruised' the clay, cleaned the flint and looked after the horse that turned the mill. Zachariah Boreman, of whom we shall hear later at Derby, the man named Willems or Wollams already mentioned, and a certain Jinks or Jenks painted seals with mottoes, while Barton himself and two men named Boyer and Snowden worked at modelling, repairing, throwing, burnishing, and polishing.

The new attitude initiated by Duesbury at Chelsea is seen in the figures, which incline much more Derbywards than to the traditions of Sprimont's Gold Anchor period. The colours are washy, especially the greens and pinks, but the rather muddy turquoise gives place to a clearer and more bluish tint. The anchor mark is often used on the wares of the period, but now it usually acquires a 'D'.

In feeling, the figures have mostly abandoned Meissen —as Meissen itself has done—in favour of the more sentimental styles of Sèvres. The new affectation is seen in the Schreiber Collection in adaptations by Etienne Falconet after designs by Boucher, such as 'La Bergère des Alpes', and 'L'Oracle, ou Le Noeud de Cravate': the Derby versions were bought by Lady Charlotte in Amsterdam, as she records, for £15 the pair: she calls them 'Proposal and Acceptance'.

In the pedestal of the charming little allegorical groups of this period such as the 'Cupid as Commerce' we see the beginnings of the Louis Seize, or neo-classical influence, which was to sweep Europe for the next few decades. It followed the excavations at Herculaneum and the publication of Sir William Hamilton's catalogues of specimens of classical art—though there were other influences at work as well.

DUESBURY AND THE NEW STYLE

Duesbury was not only not behindhand in adopting the new style; he was, as Wedgwood in pottery, in the very forefront of it. He was, in fact, much more at home in it than in the

(Left) *Plate painted by Richard Askew, with cupids* en camaieu *in pink and grey. Chelsea-Derby.* c. *1780. 8¾ in. diameter.* (Centre) *'Rodney' jug. Perhaps by Edward Withers. Dated 1782. Chelsea-Derby. 7½ in.* (Right) *Teabowl, coffee cup and saucer, all painted with a landscape and a wreath of foliage in gold and blue inside a gilt chain pattern. Mark D, Crown, crossed batons and six dots, also 'No. 86.'* c. *1800.* (All Victoria & Albert Museum.)

rococo, which he never quite succeeded in translating into English. The shapes evolved in this Chelsea-Derby period are consequently a prelude to some of the finest work of the kind in English porcelain. The body—which now followed the Chelsea bone-ash formula—was fine and the glaze soft and delicate, though much inclined to craze. Excellent painting of festoons and swags or sprigs of flowers abounds; there are also designs of urns and classical figures in grey or crimson which are as good as anything of the kind done elsewhere. Our dish from the Schreiber Collection shows a festoon of husks around an urn painted *en grisaille*, with a blue border: these are often very pleasantly used on their own in black and grey. There are also some fine striped and wavy patterns after contemporary brocades.

Several Worcester patterns were copied, notably the 'Queen's' or whorl pattern: the hop trellis patterns were also used, though these may well have been taken direct from Sèvres, where they originated.

Of the named artists probably the best-known in this period is Edward Withers, whose hand is traditionally associated with the type of flower painting on the jug shown here: it is also seen in a Rodney jug in the British Museum. Zachariah Boreman's work is seen in landscapes on large vases; and some subjects after Angelica Kauffmann are reputedly by Richard Askew. More typical of the latter's work, however, are the many cupids painted *en camaieu*, or in tones of pink.

The ground colours used in this period do not always reach the standard of, for example, the Gold Anchor. The Chelsea claret is used, but with a brownish tinge; while the mazarine blue which had had so long a life now tended to be superseded by an opaque 'Derby blue'.

Duesbury's London foreman Barton was perhaps the man who years afterwards reported to Faulkner, author of the *History of Chelsea*, that the great Dr Johnson had once tried his hand at improving the Chelsea production methods. Apparently the sage was in the habit of going across to Chelsea from Fleet Street with his housekeeper about twice a week, she carrying a basket of provisions for the day. He was not allowed to enter the mixing room—no stranger was—but was given a room of his own for mixing, and allowed access to the kilns. Unfortunately his wares always collapsed in the kiln, whereas those using the proprietor's formula came out perfectly; and the Doctor retired from the business in disgust.

Chelsea-Derby and Derby. (Left) *Vase painted in turquoise blue and gilt;* (centre) *Vase and cover painted* en grisaille *with a pierced ormolu band and goat's head handles. Derby.* c. *1790;* (Right) *Vase painted in blue and gilt, adapted from a Sèvres model known as the* vase flaçon à mouchoirs. (All Victoria & Albert Museum.)

No doubt there were a number of reasons why in 1784 Duesbury gave up the Chelsea factory altogether, removing the models and other equipment to Derby. He was approaching his sixtieth year and had gone through at least one serious illness. His partner Heath had gone bankrupt in 1780, which no doubt taxed his finances and made it difficult to maintain two establishments. But the greatest influence may well have been the fact that for the past five years Josiah Wedgwood had been enamelling nearby in Chelsea the famous creamwares which he potted at Etruria, his new factory-village in Staffordshire. These wares were already competing strongly with porcelain, and Wedgwood was not the man to baulk at stealing men—or their secrets—from other factories. In fact, when faced with the problem of gilding a tea and coffee set for Queen Charlotte, he asked his brother in London to go after one of Barton's former employees, the Jinks or Jenks mentioned above (who was now at Bow): 'If it would not be too tedious I wish you would buy a cream coloured enamelled cream ewer and get Jenks to gild all the spaces by the flowers . . . if he does it well he would perhaps tell you how it is polished . . . for a little money.'

It was clearly time for Duesbury to retire to Derby, where he had the field to himself.

Chelsea-Derby and Derby. (Left to right) *Mug with glass bottom, painted in blue and gold, c. 1780; cup, cover and saucer painted* en camaieu *in crimson and gilt (by Richard Askew?) in Sèvres style, mark D and an anchor in gold; custard cup and cover painted with cornflowers (the 'French' or 'Angoulême' sprig), c. 1800, mark D with crown and crossed batons; mug painted with wreaths and festoons of purple roses. c. 1790. (The custard cup was sold to Lady Charlotte Schreiber as 'French Fürstenburg'.) (Victoria & Albert Museum.)*

7. Crown and Bloor Derby

Having now concentrated all his activities in Derby, Duesbury dropped the Chelsea anchor mark and replaced it by that of the Crown Derby period. The crown appears over crossed batons, with a 'D' below: the initial could stand either for Duesbury or Derby—and if anyone cared to mistake it for the 'Dresden' so often mentioned in the firm's advertisements, it is unlikely that the owner of the factory would have lost much sleep over the fact.

William Duesbury did not survive the change for many years. He died in 1786 and was succeeded by a son of the same name, William Duesbury II, an industrious and able man who seems in general to have continued and even developed his father's policy.

FINE TABLE WARES

This is particularly shown in the table wares of the period, which more than fulfil the promise of the Chelsea-Derby era, and in fact may be classed among the finest achievements in English porcelain and china. One uses the two terms advisedly, for it was during this era that there were developed the new bodies which, by making increasing use of calcined bone-ash and other materials, were to evolve into the standard English bone china.

At the time of the concentration at Derby the factory was using a fine body and a rich glaze, both of which were admirably suited to painting. The fullest advantage was taken of this; and in fact a great deal of what are usually thought of as 'useful' wares were intended not for use, but for display in cabinets. A speciality in this department was the coffee 'can' and saucer: the straight-sided shape, without foot-rim, was taken from Sèvres, but the decoration was usually characteristically English. The same applied to the larger ornamental wares of the period, intended for the side table or the mantelshelf.

All this decorative effort called for a strong team of artists, and the younger Duesbury went to endless trouble to maintain such a team around him. Of the flower painters, the name of Edward Withers is associated by Haslem with the earlier styles deriving from Meissen. In the work attributed to him there is a stylized outlining to the petals, and, as in water-colours, the highlights are given by the support, in this case the fine white porcelain shining up through the enamel colours. The method is well shown in a small jug in the Schreiber Collection, also in the well-known 'Rodney' jugs of which there are specimens in both the Victoria and Albert and the British Museums. The head moulded in the spout is that of Admiral Lord Rodney (1719–92) and a medallion on the body below it commemorates that famous sailor's victory over the French commander De Grasse in the West Indies in the year 1782. According to Haslem, Withers, who was himself a convivial character, painted one of these jugs for a benefit society to which most of the artists in Derby belonged and it went the rounds at monthly meetings of the club from the date of its making down to 1862 or 1863. Perhaps it lurks unidentified still in some collector's cabinet.

Withers spent several years at Caughley and in the Staffordshire factories, but ended his life at Derby, apparently in some distress, for he was buried at the expense of his workmates.

New ground in flower-painting styles was broken by that unlucky genius William Billingsley, whose fate it was to neglect his great talents as a painter in a quest for a porcelain which would rival the exquisite soft-paste porcelain of Sèvres. The 'Billingsley' style of flower-painting, which was adopted by a wide range of painters in different factories, called for a more naturalistic treatment of subjects, especially roses: his technique consisted in washing the colour over the whole flower and modelling it by wiping out the lights with a nearly dry brush.

Billingsley had been apprenticed at Derby in 1774 and worked there for nearly twenty-five years, so that his influence on other painters in the factory must have been very strong. When he left for Pinxton in 1796 this occasioned some anxiety to Joseph Lygo, the Derby factory's agent in London. On hearing the news, he wrote to Duesbury: 'I hope you will be able to make a bargain with Mr Billingsley for him to continue with you, for it will be a great loss to lose such a hand, and not only that, but his going to another factory will put them in the way of doing flowers in the same way, which at present they are entirely ignorant of.'

But Billingsley had already been lost to the factory in spirit, for he had spent long hours in the company of Zachariah Boreman experimenting with his soft-paste formulae in the cellar of an inn. When he had evolved what he thought to be a workable body, he went off to Pinxton and other places.

Billingsley left as his memorial the exquisite but impossibly costly porcelain of Swansea and Nantgarw; but throughout his life he was hounded by creditors and dogged by personal tragedies and failures. He ended his life quietly helping John Rose at Coalport and perhaps had a hand in potting the fine wares produced there.

The characteristic 'Billingsley' bouquet of flowers, whether painted by the master himself or by a follower, has one or more rather blowsy pink roses, with passion flowers,

(Left) *Plate painted with dogs by 'Jockey' Hill, in a panel reserved on an apple green ground with gilt scrolling Mark 'D' crown and cross batons, pattern 'No. 268', in blue. 9¼ in. diameter. (Sotheby & Co.) (Right) Plate painted with fruit by Thomas Steele. Derby. c. 1830. Mark, a circular band inscribed 'Bloor Derby' enclosing a crown printed in red. 9 in. diameter. (Victoria & Albert Museum.)*

irises, yellow hollyhocks and other blooms, sometimes in long spreading sprays. Several pieces attributed to this painter are to be found in the Victoria and Albert Museum.

'QUAKER' PEGG

A quite different style of flower painting is attributed to William 'Quaker' Pegg, another of the highly individual characters who turn up so frequently in the annals of potting. Born in Staffordshire, Pegg became a fervent Calvinist at the age of eleven but nevertheless in after life deeply deplored the time he spent as a youth in attending horse races, bull-baiting at the Burslem wakes and ox-roastings at Stoke. After a spell with the Baptists he finally joined the Society of Friends, thus earning the soubriquet which followed him all his life.

Like all apprentice potters, Pegg spent his early days at the ovens, and after a fifteen-hour day he would sit up teaching himself painting from *The Artists' Repository*, a publication which came out in thirty-six parts. As he himself wrote:

Cabaret set painted with named Derbyshire landscapes by Zachariah Boreman. Mark (except on cream jug) 'D' crown and cross batons with six dots. Derby. c. 1790. (Victoria & Albert Museum.)

Worship, of whatever kind,
Oft was banished from my mind;
Then I broke my old connexions,
Placed on drawing my affections;
Dedicated all my powers
To the Arts in leisure hours.

Pegg arrived at Derby in 1796, the year of Billingsley's departure, presumably to take the older man's place. He did not, however, follow Billingsley's style but specialized in doing large, nearly life-size individual blooms with total naturalism, even showing where leaves had been eaten away by insects: it was almost the older 'botanical flowers' style. He liked to cover the whole surface, leaving room only for a narrow gilded border. He used the opaque chrome green which had superseded the translucent green from copper employed by his predecessor, and he would often write in the name of the flower.

ASKEW'S CUPIDS

As the neo-classical influence gathered momentum figure painting developed strongly. The work of the Chelsea painter Richard Askew, famous for his cupids in the Chelsea-Derby period, has already been mentioned. He seems to have come to Derby about the year 1772, and to have continued to work for the factory until 1795, but it seems likely from an agreement found by Haslem that in later years he worked from his home in Birmingham as an 'outside decorator'. Subjects of his mentioned in the Pattern Books include 'Palemon and Lavinaia' in colours on a plate

with a dark blue border; and 'Venus and Cupid' on a small mug. Askew's cupids, as Hurlbutt has pointed out, are not the conventional babies of Sèvres, but real-life youngsters, perhaps portraits of his own children. In his *camaieu* work this painter had a highly individual touch, laying on tones boldly in broad washes, as in watercolours or delftware. In his colour painting, however, where he was perhaps copying other men's work, the handling is much less assured.

Another of the figure painters was James Banford, although he was also used on birds, flowers, and landscapes. He began his career at Champion's factory in Bristol, home of the first English hard-paste, and later he worked at the Wedgwood decorating shop in Chelsea. He had the touch of the miniature painter; and very characteristic of his work is the cup from the Victoria and Albert Museum with the figure of a girl in this style.

John and Robert Brewer were artists of some repute before they started to paint on Derby china. John had been working for Duesbury in London since 1782, and some very fine paintings of shipping scenes are believed to be the work of one or other of the brothers. Perhaps it is the same hand which is to be seen in some camp scenes such as appear on the vase in the Victoria and Albert Museum collection.

Of the landscape painters at Derby, perhaps the most famous of all is that Zachariah Boreman whom we have already met in the Chelsea-Derby era. He came to Derby in 1783 with the rest of the factory and there developed quite a different style. His work is much broader in treatment, and he seems to have taken up the technique of the early watercolourists, i.e. first setting out the details in monochrome and then laying in low-toned washes. Typical of his work—and of the fine potting at Derby generally—is the cabaret set shown on p. 54. The oval panels, with their striped gilt borders, are reserved in a ground of pale pink, and each has a named Derbyshire view.

Another landscape painter who started at Chelsea was 'Jockey' Hill, so-called because of his practice of riding

(Left) *Plate painted with flowers by Leonard Lead. Derby. c. 1830. 10 in. diameter.* (Right) *Plate painted by Richard Dodson with brightly coloured birds in gilt and turquoise borders. Derby. c. 1820. Both Crown Derby mark.* (Both Victoria & Albert Museum.)

rapidly to work on a pony, his coat-tails flapping in the breeze. The loss of three fingers of his right hand did not hinder him from manipulating a brush and 'pencil'; and his work, though similar in many ways to Boreman's, uses even more meticulous stippling and hatching as well as stronger colours.

The name of George Complin is known to us only by its appearance in the pattern book, but it shows that he did a great deal of work for the factory. He seems to have specialized in fruit and birds; and Haslem indicates that although his fruit painting was conventionally Meissenesque his birds were done in bright natural colours. The same authority holds that his are the paintings where a squirrel or some other small animal is shown out of proportion to the other figures; and collectors accept this as an indication of his work.

DERBY 'BISCUIT' FIGURES

No great development was shown in the painted and glazed figures of this era: for the most part they follow the well-established routines of both factories. Quite outstanding, however, are the biscuit, or unglazed figures. Some had been made in the Chelsea-Derby period, but it was now that the class was fully developed, to become another of Derby's great achievements in ceramics.

They were, of course, inspired by the *bisque* porcelain of Sèvres, introduced about the year 1753 by Jean-Jacques Bachelier, the art director, as an alternative to the white glazed figures already in production while the factory was still at Vincennes. Madame de Pompadour was so greatly taken by the delicacy of modelling made possible with the new *materiel*, that she immediately ordered to be re-made in it a set of eight figures after Boucher which she already had in a glazed version. Etienne-Maurice Falconet, the sculptor, modelled many delightful original figures in *bisque*; there was also a whole class which were commissioned as smaller versions of monumental sculpture.

At Derby the biscuit of this early period is soft to the touch, and a 'smear' glaze produced by volatilization in the kiln gives it a most pleasant texture: it was to provide the model for the Parian ware popular in Victorian times. Many of the early figures were modelled by Jean-Jacques (or John James) Spängler, son of the director of the Zurich factory. Spängler was reputedly a wayward and unreliable character, but to judge by the work attributed to him in a list of the productions in stock in 1795 he seems to have been an excellent modeller.

Pierre Stephan was another foreign modeller of the period who is credited with some fine work—in fact Mr Savage considers that he was responsible for three groups after Angelica Kauffmann subjects—Bacchantes, Cupids and Virgins—attributed to Spängler by Haslem. His speciality, however, seems to have been the modelling of large statuettes of English admirals, generals, and other national heroes, the original models for some of which, with their names incised on the base, still exist. They include the 'Lord Howe' in the British Museum and figures from a set of 'Elements' in the Victoria and Albert Museum.

Some figures are in dispute between Pierre Stephan and William Coffee, who started life as a furnace-man at Coade's factory in Lambeth, where the well-known architectural Coade-stone figures were produced. There is a 'Shepherd' in the Victoria and Albert Museum which is usually attributed to him: the clay model for it is in the Nottingham Castle Museum —which has a companion 'Shepherdess' by Stephan. Lygo seems to have recruited him for Derby, not as a modeller but as a kilnman;

Biscuit figure of a Shepherd, modelled by William Coffee (see this page). (Victoria & Albert Museum.)

and at one time he was making porcelain in a small factory in Derby in partnership with 'Billy' Duesbury, a namesake and relative of William Duesbury II.

In his 'Shepherd' Coffee was made to follow the Derby practice of first modelling the figure in the nude and then clothing it, which is one of the reasons why the modelling there is often more anatomically correct than at Chelsea. In this case he had been given a plaster cast of Adonis bought by Duesbury at a sale of the effects of the painter Joseph Wright of Derby: he then draped the figure, added a sheep, and put into his hand a shepherd's hat which, as Haslem comments, he mercifully did not allow the god to put on his very classical head. But this is a fine piece of work, and an astonishing *tour de force* for a man of Coffee's origins. Lygo, however, found Coffee's modelling not altogether to his taste. He wrote to Duesbury: 'I do not much admire Mr Coffee's modelling from what I have seen. The Figure No. 359 is very vulgar about the bosom, for sure never such bubbys were seen and so much exposed.' Later in life Coffee left Derby to take up terra-cotta modelling, and in the end he emigrated to America.

It will have been noticed that several of the older hands left the factory around the year 1795. In fact William Duesbury II had had to relax his control at this time. He had put a great deal of effort into the factory's work, and set up standards which it was never again to achieve; but he paid for this with the loss of his health, and in 1796 he died. He had appointed as manager an Irishman named Michael Kean, a successful miniature painter, but it is inferred that Duesbury's team did not get on with their new master.

At this time the body moved even closer towards the new bone china, becoming harder and whiter: the glaze and the enamels, instead of sinking into it, stood out on the surface, and therefore tended to flake off with use.

Kean married Duesbury's widow in 1798, and for some years the firm carried on as Duesbury and Kean: the mark occasionally shows a monogram 'D' and 'K' with the crown

Derby china picture, one of a pair, painted with garden flowers, including stocks, roses, delphiniums, auriculas, etc.; the frame moulded with shells and acanthus leaves. 9¾ by 11¼ in. (Sotheby & Co.)

and crossed batons. The new Duesbury was William III, eldest son of William II, who was ten years old at his father's death: but on the evidence of his sister he never, even at maturity, took an active part in the family business. In the year 1811 Kean separated from his wife and left the town.

BLOOR TAKES OVER

The business was sold to Robert Bloor, who for some years had been the book-keeper. His was an unenviable heritage. The Napoleonic wars had left the nation exhausted, and English manufacturers had been virtually cut off from the export markets which they had been steadily building up on the Continent. Bloor had to take over enormous quantities of undecorated porcelain; faced with the need to pay off the Duesbury family as quickly as possible, he brought out all these old stocks—'firsts' and 'seconds' indiscriminately—and had them decorated by a new team of painters.

It was presumably because of their uneven quality that he covered a great many of them with heavy, often tasteless versions of the old Imari patterns—nothing could be better devised to hide defects. But it was a sad falling off for a firm which had been producing domestic wares of distinction.

Nevertheless Bloor did make a genuine effort at quality productions, gathering round him painters capable of meeting the current taste for highly detailed naturalistic work in the style of the oil painting of the day.

There was Thomas Steele, perhaps the finest fruit painter of his time, together with his sons Edwin and Horatio; Leonard Lead also worked in this *genre*, using a rather mannered style; while the flower painting of Moses Webster, a pupil of the famous Thomas Baxter, inclined to hark back to the more naturalistic feeling: much of his later work has a wind-blown or 'washed-out' appearance.

George Robertson specialized in landscape: he had been brought in to fill one of the empty places in the exodus of 1795 and he worked well on into the Bloor period. Some of the work attributed to him is to be seen in the Victoria and Albert Museum, as is that of another landscape man, Jesse Mountford. William Corden combined landscapes with figure painting—there are scenes from Tegg's edition of Shakespeare and portraits in the manner of contemporary oils.

But this work appears much more appropriately on the plaques and porcelain pictures which were made in the last decades of the factory. John Haslem, whose writings we have been quoting throughout this account, painted a great many of these, and employed upon them a style which he was to put to good use later as a miniaturist and painter on enamel: he was engaged at one time on portraits for the royal family.

Richard Dodson, working at the factory from 1815 to 1825, painted brightly coloured birds, usually in watery landscapes; and rather more fanciful work in gold on a coloured ground, usually dark blue, was done by William Watson.

Haslem mentions other names, but so far it has been difficult to identify their work. There was William Cotton, who is said to have painted landscapes and occasionally Dutch genre subjects. Some grotesque painting on large beer mugs taken from engravings by John Collier is said to be by William Dixon. Daniel Lucas was a prolific landscape man who also painted public-house signs in Derby.

In 1828 Robert Bloor became mentally deranged, and the factory was carried on for his family by James Thomason, the commercial manager, who was John Haslem's uncle. Bloor died in 1845, and Thomas Clarke, a maltster, who had married Bloor's granddaughter, gradually closed down the business. The equipment was sold, and the moulds, many of them from the Chelsea days, eventually passed into the hands of the Copelands, the still-surviving successors to the Spodes.

Although the old company ended its days in 1848, potting continued elsewhere in Derby. A group of former employees, including William Locker and Sampson Hancock, set up in King Street, and continued under the style of 'The Old Crown Derby China Works' until well into the present century.

In the meantime a group of business-men, led by Edward Philips from Worcester, started in 1876 in the Osmaston Road the business which in 1890 became the Royal Crown Derby Porcelain Company. In 1935 it took over the older concern in King Street, and continues in existence.

Derby china plaque painted by John Haslem. Mark, a crossed swords in blue. c. 1833–40. $9\frac{7}{8}$ by 7 in.
(Victoria & Albert Museum.)

8. Marks

1. *Chelsea. The incised triangle, 1745–50.*

2. *Raised Anchor (in relief on an applied medallion, the anchor sometimes picked out in red), c. 1749–53.*

3. *Crown and trident, in underglaze blue, c. 1745–50.*

4. *Anchor, mostly in red, but also in underglaze blue, and blue or purple enamel (overglaze), c. 1752–6.*

5. *Chelsea-Derby, in gold or red, c. 1770–84.*

6. *Derby. In blue purple or gold, c. 1780–84.*

7. *In gold, 1770–80.*

8. *Model numbers on figures, 1770–80.*

9. *In blue crimson or purple, c. 1784–1810.*

10. *Duesbury and Kean period, in blue crimson or purple, c. 1795.*

11. *c. 1790.*

12. *Bloor period, printed in red, c. 1811–48.*

64